blueallrise

blueallrise

official blue product

CONTENDER BOOKS

A division of the Contender Entertainment Group

**Interviews and text by
Jordan Paramor**

**Blue is managed by Daniel Glatman
for Intelligent Music Management Ltd.**

First published 2002 by Contender Books
48 Margaret Street
London W1W 8SE
www.contendergroup.com

This edition published 2002
1 3 5 7 9 10 8 6 4 2

ISBN 1 84357 018 1

Design by designsection, Frome, Somerset
Repro by Radstock Repro, Midsomer Norton, Bath
Printed and bound in Great Britain by Butler & Tanner Ltd, Frome and London
Concept by Alison Parker
Production by Rebecca Gee

contents

helloandwelcome

...to the first ever official Blue book!

Inside you can get the lowdown on the four of us, find out all about our schooldays, what we really think about fame and each other, and even what we think of our fans.

We've had a wicked first year, and this is only the beginning. We really couldn't have done it without all of you, so thanks to all of our fans for being there, and here's to a brilliant future!

WORK HARD BE
GOOD LOVE

Simon
x

TAKE CARE
Love

Lee
X

All the Best,
with ♡
Dunk
x

BEST WISHES
WITH LOVE

Antony
xx

8

What was your favourite member of Blue like as a young boy? Did they behave themselves at school? And how do they feel about being in Blue? You can find all the answers here!

Full name:	Antony Daniel Costa
DOB:	23/6/1981
Height:	5' 8"
Brothers and sisters:	1 brother and 1 sister
From:	Edgware, Middlesex
Hair colour:	Dark Brown / Black
Eye colour:	Dark Brown
Star sign:	Cancer

antonyprofile

> **"The worst trouble I got into at school was when I bit this kid because he took my clothes peg."**

IN THE BEGINNING

There's no doubting Antony has got one of the cheekiest smiles in pop, so you won't be surprised to hear that he had a naughty streak in his younger days.

"I was quite naughty when I was growing up for the first three years because I was an only child. I'm three years older than my sister so I was really spoilt and always got my own way.

My first memory as a kid is walking into primary school on my first day when I was about five. My mum was holding my hand because I didn't know where to go, and I started crying because I didn't want her to leave. I remember starting to play with these kids and then she left, and suddenly I was fine. I'll never forget that."

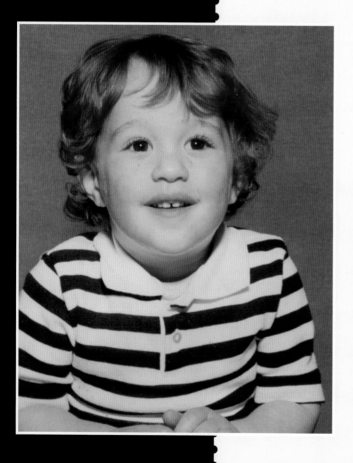

SCHOOL DAYS

Antony's mischievous streak carried on until his school days, but thankfully he soon grew out of, er, biting people.

"When I first started school I was really naughty and I used to bite people all the time, but I stopped that pretty quickly. I couldn't exactly go round doing it now! I think if you're naughty as a kid then you learn the hard way, and you learn to be more respectful as you grow up. I know loads of people who were really good kids and have gone off the rails now that they're older.

The worst trouble I got into at school was when I bit this kid because he took my clothes peg. We all used to have different symbols above the clothes pegs like rabbits and dogs and umbrellas, and I wanted a dog. But he took the last one so we ended up having a fight. It was really bad. My three mates and I used to pretend we were in *The A Team* as well. We'd walk into classrooms and cause havoc. We were terrible.

I enjoyed school because I met all my mates there and I had a laugh. I used to enjoy doing drama and music, but apart from that I hated everything. I really hated science and maths. My school reports used to say that I could be quite chatty and distracting to other pupils, but I was a good student. I didn't cause problems all the time, I just used to chat all the time and make my mates talk to me, so I got into trouble. I suppose I was the cheeky one."

Antony shares his band-mates' love of acting and has appeared in *The Bill*, *Grange Hill* and BBC sitcom *Chalk*, and even got the chance to show off his performance skills on the legendary Cilla Black show *Surprise, Surprise*.

"I was always in the school plays. I was in *Dick Whittington* once playing one of his mates, which was brilliant. And when I was older I was in the play *Cabaret* and got to play Danny Zuco in *Grease*, which I loved because it

was my favourite film of all time. It was just amazing,
I loved John Travolta.

Everyone knows by now that my mum set me up to
go on *Surprise, Surprise* and I got to sing and dance
as Danny in *Grease* alongside Sonia! That was my first
real taste of fame. It was great and if it wasn't for my
mum that would never have happened."

BOY IN BLUE

Despite initially planning to become an actor, big 90s
pop bands like Take That and East 17 inspired Antony
to sing: "I never actually decided that I wanted to be
a pop star. I used to like a lot of bands in the days
of Take That, and I was a big Robbie and East 17 fan.
I always thought: 'I wouldn't mind doing that', but
acting was my first love.

Being a pop star didn't dawn on me for a long time because I went through a stage when my voice was breaking and I couldn't sing at all. But now I absolutely love being in Blue. I was in a band before that was really cheesy, whereas we're not at all. I get guys in clubs coming up and shaking my hand and stuff, which is really unusual if you're in what's considered to be a 'boy band'.

I'd like to be in this business for as long as possible because to me it's the best thing in the world. I can never see myself being sat behind a desk from nine to five."

13

Ant questionsand

What did we find out about Antony? That he owns 25 pairs of jeans, can't cook, and collects *Only Fools and Horses* memorabilia. Oh, and a whole lot more...

What did you get for your last birthday?
A DKNY watch from my mum and dad.

Do you give to charity?
Now we're an established band we're going to try and do a lot for charity and for the homeless. I'd like to do a lot of stuff for cancer and AIDS.

Cats or dogs?
Both.

Who was the last person you spoke to on the phone?
My mum and dad.

What's your worst household chore?
I can't work the washing machine, so it's that.

answers

How do you end your phone calls?
"See ya later, bye".

What did you dream about last night?
I dreamt the boys and I went to Asia and we got into trouble with these gangs. I'd watched *Rush Hour 2* and it was on my mind so it gave me weird dreams.

Do you read your horoscope?
Yeah, Duncan's got me really into them. I'm a Cancerian so I'm home-loving, sensitive, and kind.

How long does it take you to get ready for a night out?
20 minutes.

Who do you admire?
Apart from my parents, George Michael. He's my idol.

"Never give up, because you'll get there."

Do you read poetry?
No.

What book changed your life?
The Commitments. It's such a brilliant but sad story that shows you that bands don't last forever. Unless you're Status Quo.

What was the last thing you cooked?
I don't cook, sorry.

What time do you sleep in until when you've got a day off?
I try not to sleep in because we don't get much time off and I want to see my mates and go shopping.

What's the weirdest rumour you've heard about yourself?

That I was dating Jessica from Liberty. We just laughed.

What's in your fridge?

This morning it was smoked salmon, cream cheese, orange juice, and some fruit and vegetables.

What's in your pockets?

My phone – which is my life – and my wallet.

When did you last laugh until you cried?

When I watched *Rush Hour 2* yesterday, it had me in stitches.

Favourite catchphrase?

"I would" and "bothered".

What was the first single you ever bought?

Pray by Take That. I pretended it was for my sister.

Do you have a secret ambition?

I'd like to play for Tottenham for a day.

What's the most romantic thing you've ever done?
Bought a girl after-dinner mints. It was two and half years ago and I was skint. I just had enough to get the bus to see her and buy her the mints.

What's your duvet like?
It used to be a Tottenham one, but now it's plain white.

What aftershave do you wear?
Emporio Armani and 212 for men.

What sport are you best at?
Football.

How many Valentine's cards did you get last year?
Two.

"I would most like to work with George Michael and Robbie Williams."

Favourite film?
Grease.

Favourite TV show?
Only Fools and Horses.

Do you collect anything?
Only Fools and Horses memorabilia. I've got all the videos, books, scripts, Del's chain and aftershave, Trotters Independent Traders teapot, an alarm clock, and I'm collecting the DVDs.

What questions are you bored of answering?
"Do you like being called a boy band?"

Which five people – dead or alive – would you invite to your fantasy dinner party?
Elvis Presley, George Michael, Robbie Williams, Madonna, and the whole of the Spurs team!

What's the best advice you've ever been given by anyone?
My uncle used to be a professional footballer and he told me never to give up, because you'll get there.

What's your all time favourite song?
Careless Whisper by George Michael because I had my first slow dance to it. The girl ended up being my girlfriend.

Where do you buy your clothes?
French Connection, Diesel and Levi's.

Who would you most like to work with?
George Michael and Robbie Williams. That would be an amazing combination.

Where did you go on your last holiday?
On a Caribbean cruise. Duncan and I took our families.

Are you allergic to anything?
No.

What's your biggest extravagance?
Jeans, I've got about 25 pairs.

All Rise!

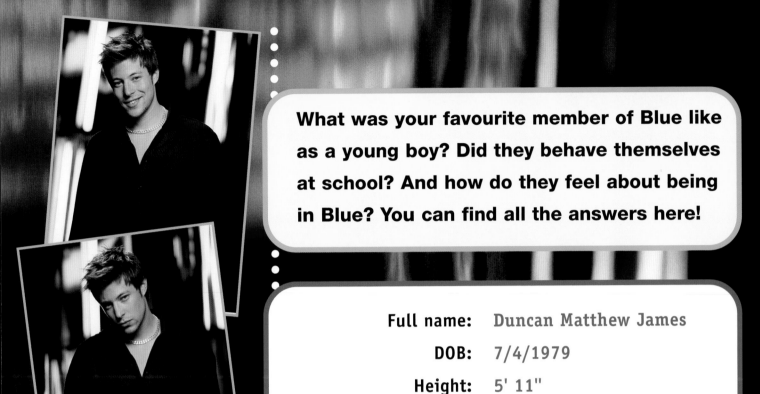

What was your favourite member of Blue like as a young boy? Did they behave themselves at school? And how do they feel about being in Blue? You can find all the answers here!

Full name:	Duncan Matthew James
DOB:	7/4/1979
Height:	5' 11"
Brothers and sisters:	None
From:	Devon and Dorset
Hair colour:	Light Brown / Blond
Eye colour:	Blue
Star sign:	Aries

duncanprofile

IN THE BEGINNING

Duncan describes his childhood as idyllic, but his first memory is far from it!

"Growing up as a kid I was very loved by my mum and my grandparents. I was brought up by the three of them. I've never had a father, so my grandparents did my father's job. My earliest memory was when I was about three and my grandparents had this Alsatian. My gran always warned me not to crawl around the floor when it was around, but one day I did and it nipped me on the eye. I was crying my eyes out and it had to be put down the next day because it was too much of a risk for it to be around me.

My other very early memory is of going to playschool with my gran. I remember kicking up a fuss and screaming, and she had to stay with me for the whole day. I don't think I went back to playschool after that because I hated it so much."

SCHOOL DAYS

Duncan's smile is a winner with fans and their mums across the nation these days, so it's hardly surprising that even as a young lad he won his teachers' hearts.

"I made loads of friends at school and was always quite a good lad. I had a sweet angelic face and a smile that could get away with murder! I would get into trouble but always get away with it. My best mate was a guy called Robert and he was really naughty. He would come up with the idea of doing bad stuff and then make me do it. But the teachers

"I knew from an early age that I wanted to be in the entertainment business."

24

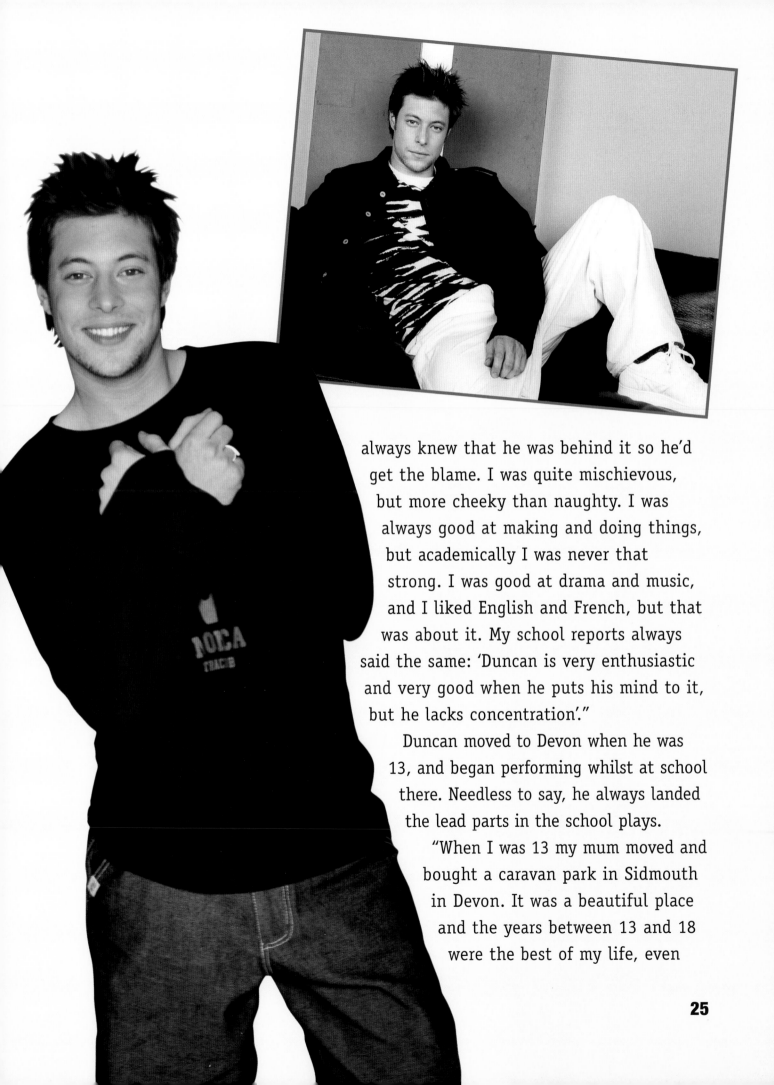

always knew that he was behind it so he'd get the blame. I was quite mischievous, but more cheeky than naughty. I was always good at making and doing things, but academically I was never that strong. I was good at drama and music, and I liked English and French, but that was about it. My school reports always said the same: 'Duncan is very enthusiastic and very good when he puts his mind to it, but he lacks concentration'."

Duncan moved to Devon when he was 13, and began performing whilst at school there. Needless to say, he always landed the lead parts in the school plays.

"When I was 13 my mum moved and bought a caravan park in Sidmouth in Devon. It was a beautiful place and the years between 13 and 18 were the best of my life, even

though I missed my grandparents a lot. I was always lucky enough to get the lead parts in school plays because I loved drama, and my drama teacher also got me into the Youth Theatre, which was fantastic. I remember doing the amateur theatre premier production of *The Young Sherlock Holmes*, and I played Dr. Watson. I loved it. I eventually left Sidmouth when I was 18 to start my career. I knew from an early age that I wanted to be in the entertainment business."

BOY IN BLUE

Duncan got his first taste of the entertainment business as a redcoat for Haven Holidays, and he says that his time there taught him an incredible amount and provided the perfect springboard for his showbiz career.

"My first job with Haven Holidays was as a male vocalist for their site at West Bay. It was great because it was in between my mum and my grandparents so I could go and visit them on alternate weekends. One day some people from head office came down and heard me sing and were really blown away, so they transferred me to their camp on the Isle of

"Everything has gone so well and things just keep getting better and better for us."

Wight where I got to sing a lot more. Whilst I was there, head office came to see me again and told me they wanted to put me in the most prestigious site for Haven Mates. To be asked to go there was a big honour and the quality of performers was amazing. I learnt so much and I see the years I spent at Haven as my university years. I learnt more than I ever could have done at college."

As much as he loved his time with Haven, Duncan was soon ready to move on to bigger and better things.

"I saw an advert for a boy band in *The Stage* magazine, and I auditioned and got in. Zac from Northern Line was also in the band, and I moved to London and stayed with the group for just under a year. But in the end I decided it wasn't really for me. Blue came about a bit later. I knew the other lads from the audition circuit, and basically none of us was really happy with what we were doing, so we decided to form our own band. We met our manager, Daniel Glatman, and next thing we knew we were being signed to Innocent Records. It was just incredible. Everything has gone so well and things just keep getting better and better for us."

Dunk questions

We fired tons of questions at Duncan and discovered that he admires his mum, always reads his horoscopes, and once got 14 Valentine's cards!

What did you get for your last birthday?
I got a Gucci wallet, a silver ring, some money, and my mum got me some stuff for my house.

Do you give to charity?
Yes.

Cats or dogs?
Dogs, definitely.

What do you think about most often?
I think a lot about everything. I think about my grandparents a lot.

Who was the last person you spoke to on the phone?
My mum.

andanswers

"You only get one life so go for what you want and not what other people want you to do."

What's your worst household chore?
Washing up. I hate it.

How do you end your phone calls?
It's usually "see you in a bit". Or if it's my mum it's "love you mum, bye".

What did you dream about last night?
I dreamt these people were trying to kill us all and I had to try and shoot them, but when they turned blue it was impossible to kill them. It was very odd. It was more like a nightmare.

Do you read your horoscope?
Yes, always.

How long does it take you to get ready for a night out?

I have a soak in the bath, iron my clothes, and then sort my barnet out. I reckon about 45 minutes to an hour.

Who do you admire?
I admire my mum for everything she's been through in her life. I admire every single parent who has to bring up a kid on his or her own. I was lucky I had my grandparents to help bring me up. I also admire inner strength in people.

Do you read poetry?

Yes.

What book changed your life?

I don't read a lot of books, but the *Harry Potter* series changed me because I couldn't put them down. It's the most books I've ever read in my life.

What was the last thing you cooked?

I love cooking, I'd love to be a chef. I love cooking roasts, so it was probably that.

What time do you sleep in until when you've got a day off?

I sleep as long as possible. I can stay up all night but I can't wake up at all. I'm terrible in the morning.

What's in your fridge?

Milk, butter, cheese, orange juice, eggs, bacon – the real basics.

When did you last laugh until you cried?

At my mate's birthday party recently.

Favourite catchphrase?

"In a bit" or "spinning out".

What was the first single you ever bought?

Kylie Minogue's *I Should Be So Lucky*. I'm a huge fan.

What's in your pockets?

My phone, my wallet, and my keys.

Do you have a secret ambition?
I'd love to play the main part in the musical *Godspell*. And I'd love to be in a Hollywood movie.

What's the most romantic thing you've ever done?
When I was about nine I had a huge crush on a girl down the street and I saved up all my pocket money and bought her chocolates and roses for Valentine's Day. I even sent her a letter saying I loved her. I never got to go out with her, but we're mates now.

What's your motto for life?
"You only get one life so go for what you want and not what other people want you to do. And if you're determined enough, you can do whatever you want".

Do you believe in aliens?
Yes.

What's your duvet like?
It's full of bright colours like oranges and reds and yellows.

What aftershave do you wear?
Gucci Rush, Davidoff Cool Water and Fahrenheit.

What sport are you best at?
Tennis.

How many Valentine's cards did you get last year?
Five. I got 14 one year, that's my best.

Favourite film?
The Matrix and *The Fifth Element*.

Favourite TV show?
Friends and *Star Trek Voyager*.

What questions are you bored of answering?
"How did you all get together?"

Which five people – dead or alive – would you invite to your fantasy dinner party?
My grandparents, my mum, Michael Jackson so I could look at him, and Britney Spears because I fancy the pants off her.

What's your favourite Blue song?
All Rise.

Where do you buy your clothes?
Anywhere, I'm not fussy. I'm not into big flashy labels, but I do like flares and big shirts. I'm into retro stuff, so I guess retro shops are my favourite.

Where did you go on your last holiday?
Antony and I took our families on a Caribbean cruise.

Are you allergic to anything?
No.

All Rise!

dishingthedirt!

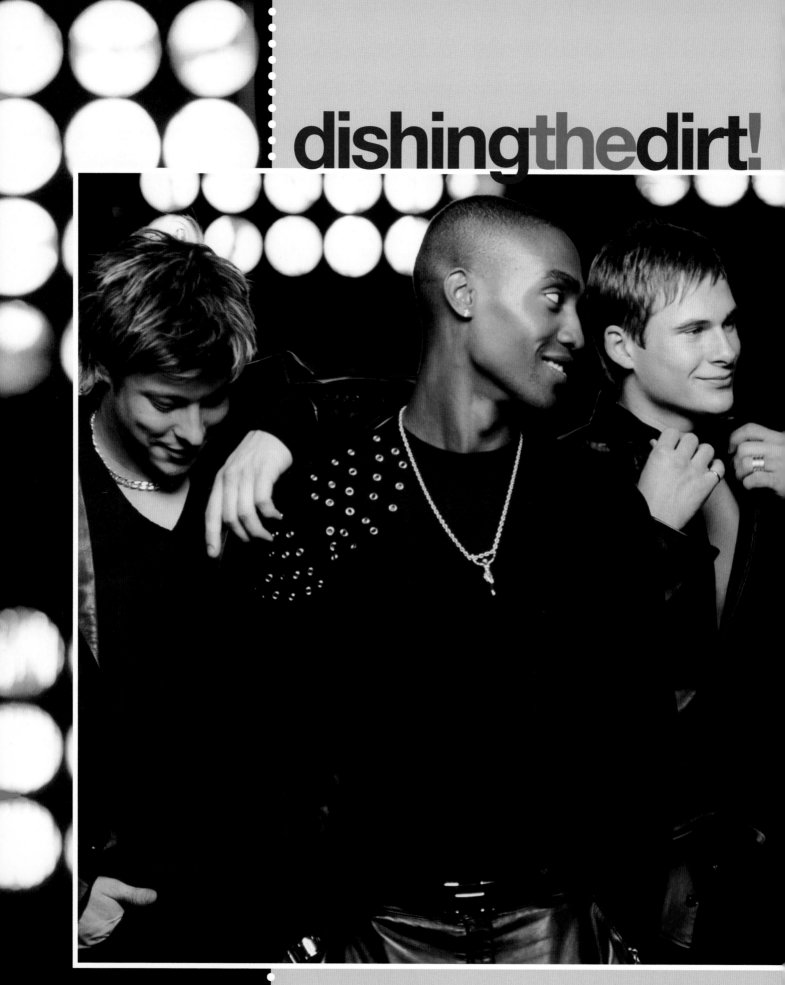

There are times when the lads from Blue are together 24/7, and there's no doubting they're the best of mates. But how willing are they to spill the beans on each other? Surprisingly willing, actually...

antony

on his band mates...

Duncan: Dunk's very hard working. He has his mad moments sometimes and he goes off on one and starts talking madly in this weird voice. I can't explain it, but he makes me laugh!

Lee: Lee is nuts. He has his quiet moments when he's tired, but not for long. He's pretty non-stop.

Simon: They're all easy to talk to, but Simon is very easy to talk to about life and girls and stuff. And he's also a hard worker. I would say Simon is the cool one, I'm the cheeky one, Lee is the young cute one, and Duncan is the sensitive one.

"...we have a lot in common to do with our thoughts on the afterlife and what happens after we die."

duncan

on his band mates...

Antony: You can't say anything bad about him, Antony is just a lovely bloke. He's different to how he used to be, he's become a lot more confident. Before he was always eager to please everyone and didn't want to upset anyone, but now he's looking after himself more. He's quite a different Ant! He stands up for himself more, which is good.

Lee: Lee is very hyperactive, but at the same time he's got a very imaginative brain that I really respect him for. His sense of awareness and perception on life is really great and we have a lot in common to do with our thoughts on the afterlife and what happens after we die. I talk to him more about that than anyone else in the band. He's a very in-depth person, and he also likes to wind you up. He's an interesting character and he intrigues me. You never know what he's going to do next.

Simon: Me and Si come from very different backgrounds and very different walks of life, and yet we get on really well and there's a lot of respect between us. We understand each other and he's a very cool guy. He's really talented and is an incredible songwriter. He makes me laugh and is probably more on my wavelength than anyone else.

lee *on his band mates...*

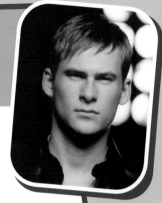

Antony: Antony is a really nice bloke and he's cheeky and funny. He goes with the flow and he's always ready for everything. He's always got his stuff laid out ready for the next morning, with his trousers folded neatly and stuff. Simon's the same, whereas Duncan and I will be the ones panicking and throwing our clothes on and chucking stuff into our suitcases at the last minute.

Duncan: Duncan and I get on well and he's really on my wavelength. We do this thing where we go crazy and jump up and down. If people saw us they'd think we were mad. But sometimes we just go off on one and we have a laugh.

Simon: Simon is the cool one. He's the oldest and he's pretty laid back. He's organised, efficient, good at getting things done, and generally a really good bloke.

simon *on his band mates...*

Antony: Antony is a cheeky chappy and is dead funny. He's pretty laid back and doesn't worry too much about things. There isn't one person I'll go to if I've got a problem, it's just whoever is around really, and all the lads are good to talk to.

Duncan: Duncan is headstrong and knows what he wants, but he's a little bit sensitive and he worries a lot. I think we've got quite a lot in common.

Lee: Lee is the youngest and he's full of energy and bubbly. He very rarely stops and he's always up for a laugh. I think we're all very individual people and we've got a lot of respect for each other.

According to the lads, Lee's got the worst chat-up lines, Antony is the biggest party animal, older women love Duncan, and Simon can't stop spending money. And that's only the half of it!

Who is the most argumentative out of all of you?

Simon: I think we can all be argumentative. We never have rows though, we have discussions and there are never raised voices.

Antony: We all bicker sometimes, but over stupid stuff like dance moves. I think it depends on what mood we're in.

Lee: It definitely depends on our mood, I don't think any of us are bad. We just bicker every now and again if we're tired or whatever. I do like winding Duncan up sometimes though, because he really bites. It's a laugh.

Duncan: Ant's not at all argumentative, but me, Lee and Si can be, so I guess it's us three.

Who's the funniest member of the band?

Antony: It depends. Lee makes me laugh a lot.

Duncan: Antony's very funny, but I also find Si funny. Lee can be quite funny as well because he doesn't care what he says.

Lee: Antony.

Simon: Antony has everyone in stitches, and he's a joke teller whereas I'll tell stories. But I can tell funny stories!

Who has the worst chat-up lines?

Antony: Lee's quite blatant. He'll say: "You're fit, do you want to go out with me?".

Duncan: Lee, without a doubt.

Lee: Probably me, I am really blatant.

Simon: Lee, definitely.

Who's the most manic?

Duncan: Lee, he's non-stop.

Antony: Lee and Duncan together.

Simon: Lee.

Lee: I'd say I am. Sometimes I have to go somewhere and chill out and have a quiet moment. I've got a lot of energy.

Who's the vainest?

Lee: I don't think any of us are really vain, but we all take care over our appearance.

Duncan: Lee, Ant and I are pretty bad with our hair, we can take ages. And Si is vain in that he does his nails and puts on moisturiser.

Antony: All of them in a different way. Si takes a long time to get ready, Lee likes to look in the mirror, and Duncan will be on the phone and doing his hair without even realising.

Simon: I think everyone likes to look good and look their best, but we're not vain. We don't dress up when we're travelling or anything.

Who spends the most money?

Antony: Si.

Simon: Me and Lee. We can shop anytime.

Lee: I think it would be me and Simon. I love shopping and I never get bored with it. I just get skint.

Duncan: We all spend but Antony is probably the best. I'm terrible with money and before the band I was really in debt from spending non-stop.

Who's the most serious member of Blue?

Lee: Not me!

Duncan: Probably me, I'm quite serious. I don't find conventional things funny, I find strange things funny.

Antony: Si can be, but not in a horrible way. He just gets on with things.

Simon: Me probably. I like to get things done. But when it's time to get cracking on something, everyone can be serious.

Who's the messiest?

Duncan: Lee, definitely, closely followed by me.

Antony: Lee. You can't share a hotel room with him because he's so messy. One shoe will be in one corner of the room and another will be in another. It's a nightmare.

Simon: Lee really is very messy, but he's getting better now. Ant is the most tidy, without a doubt.

Lee: Me. I've always been messy ever since I was young. I always had loads of stuff shoved under my bed and all over the place.

Who's the biggest party animal?

Duncan: Antony I reckon. Me and him can go out together and have a wicked night. Si is the one that goes home early, and Lee will go off in his own world and do his own thing, but he does like parties.

Antony: Me and Si, we both like going out.

Simon: Antony. I'm a party animal to a certain extent, but I like to be rested for work the next day.

Lee: Antony. I'll be the first to leave a party and he'll be the last.

Who's the most successful with girls?

Lee: All of us.

Duncan: Si doesn't have to do anything. I get the older women for some reason. It must be the way I come across, and apparently when I smile the mums seem to like it. I think we all do alright though!

Antony: Me. I get most girls' numbers. We shark each other a lot, which means if I'm chatting to a girl and I walk off for a minute, one of the other guys will move in and I'm out of the picture. We muck about like that.

Simon: I think Antony is the most successful. He makes girls laugh.

Who's the kindest?

Antony: All of them. They'd all give you their last fiver.

Simon: We're all generous and we all give without expecting anything back. I think that's why we're such a good team.

Lee: I suppose all of us are. We all look out for each other and help each other out.

Duncan: Lee's very generous. If he sees a beggar in the street he'll give them 10 or 20 quid, whereas I'll give them a couple of quid. He's very kind.

Who's the laziest?

Antony: Lee can be sometimes, but our tour manager sorts us out now.

Duncan: Me and Lee are always late. Si will get somewhere about three minutes late, I'll be there ten minutes late, Lee's a half-an-hour man, and Antony's always dead on time.

Simon: Lee. I'm alright, but I've realised now that I can get away with getting ready while my car is waiting outside so I've started doing that a lot.

Lee: But none of us are really lazy. Even if we're really tired we'll do what we've got to do.

fame!

One day Antony, Lee, Simon and Duncan were four down-to-earth lads in a band, the next they were one of the biggest pop acts in the country. So how do they feel about fame? What have been their most amazing experiences so far? And what do they really think of their fans?

What are the best and worst things about fame?

Antony: The best thing is that you get to do interviews, go on TV, and travel the world. But you don't get as much sleep as you'd like to, and you don't see your family and friends enough. I'm always on the phone so my mobile bills are about £300 a month.

Duncan: The best thing is that you get a lot of things given to you, and you also get to stay in nice hotels and stuff. I suppose the fickleness of fame is one of the worst things because you don't know who to trust, and you have to be careful what you do because people are always watching you.

Lee: The best thing is getting to sing and do what I've always wanted to do for a living. The worst is all the fakeness.

Simon: The best thing is that you get really nice clothes and stuff for free. The worst thing is that everyone thinks it's easy. Everyone thinks you go to a TV show for 20 minutes and then you spend the rest of the time partying, when in reality you're working 20-hour days.

Where are the best places you've visited with the band?

Antony: Every place is nice, but I really loved Australia. It's wicked over there.

Duncan: Australia. I love seeing all the different lifestyles in places.

Lee: I'd say Italy, I absolutely love it. And also Australia.

Simon: Yep, Australia is wicked.

How do you get on with your fans?

Lee: We get on really well with them and we don't put on a cheesy false image, we're just ourselves. We also try to look after them. We're always happy to see them, but we always make sure that they're not in danger. We'd hate them to be out without their parents knowing and for them to be worried about them or whatever. We always tell them to be safe and that they can always see us another day.

Antony: They're so cool. I get sent loads of brilliant things by fans, they're fantastic.

Simon: They're always really respectful of us.

Duncan: Our fans are great, I think they're the best. They're so supportive and so kind and do so many nice things for us. They send us amazing pictures and collages, and I also get the odd pair of knickers thrown at me on stage, which is a bit weird!

What has been your most amazing performing experience to date?

Duncan: All of it.

Simon: There have been so many...

Antony: Performing at Party in the Park. Those three minutes performing *All Rise* in front of 140,000 people was just incredible. They all had their hands in the air and it was amazing.

Lee: It's weird because as soon as I get off stage I forget about it. It's like I'm a robot when I'm out there, I'm in a world of my own. It's an amazing feeling.

Do you think you've changed as a person since being in Blue?

Lee: I hate to say it but I have changed and I can't do the same things I used to do. I'm in a different environment now and work is my life. I'm still me though, I haven't changed in a bad way. Sometimes I get upset because I can't see my mates and family as much, and sometimes when my mates invite me out to a club it's really difficult because all it takes is for someone to start on me and that's it. I just hope people don't think that I think I'm too good because that's not the case at all.

Antony: I've had to grow up quite a bit and stand on my own two feet in the big wide world. I've also learnt not to take things too seriously and enjoy life. And I've also learnt that you should never believe your own hype because that's when you'll go downhill.

Duncan: I don't think fame has changed me, but it's made me more aware of the people around me. I'm still the same person, I still have the same friends, but I think I've become more cautious and more about looking after number one instead of worrying about other people all the time.

Simon: I think my appearance has changed, and I've become more businesslike because things have got to get done. And I've got more ambition now, I've got a lot of goals.

How has your relationship with the rest of the band changed since you started out?

Antony: We've got closer together and we get on better.

Simon: I think we've just got stronger. We were mates anyway so it's cool.

Duncan: Nothing's changed really. Actually, I think Antony has changed. Not in a bad way, he's just become more confident within himself.

Lee: It's all good. We'd been mates for ages and I guess we just know each other better now.

What's been your proudest moment in the band so far?

Antony: Every day is a proud moment, but I think winning the Best Newcomer award at the *Smash Hits* Poll Winners Party was the best for me. I'd been watching it on TV for years.

Simon: The first time I saw us on *Top of the Pops*. I've grown up watching it and it was amazing.

Lee: I think signing our deal, that was just incredible. It was so weird sitting in our record company with these contracts in front of us, it didn't seem real. It's amazing.

Duncan: I've had so many proud moments. The BRIT Awards were amazing, and doing Party in the Park was incredible. Being in Blue is just the best thing.

What do you miss doing most that you can't do now you're famous?

Antony: Going out with my mates.

Lee: Yeah, going out clubbing with my mates, having a kebab, and getting into trouble. I can't do that any more. It's hard because I have to be careful where I go now.

Duncan: Just normal, everyday things.

Simon: Nothing, I still go on buses and tubes and everything. But people do look at me a lot as if to say: "What are you doing here?"

Do you get recognised a lot?

Antony: Yeah, but it's wicked. People say really nice things about our music and it's really nice to hear it. I get such a buzz from it and it means all the hard work is paying off.

Simon: Yeah I do, and I spin out. It's really weird. But people are really nice, so it's all good.

What do you do when you get time off from being in the spotlight?

Antony: Shop and talk on the phone. But not as much as Duncan as he's constantly on the phone.

Duncan: I catch up with friends and family.

Simon: I sleep as much as I can.

Lee: I like to stay in and chill. It's nice to stay in and sit on the sofa with my family and watch TV because I don't get a chance to do that very often.

Do you enjoy the showbiz parties?

Antony: Oh yes. I went to Andrez from Damage's party last year and you had to dress up in school uniform, it was wicked. I quite like doing the party thing.

Simon: I love going to the parties. I went to a really good S Club 7 party once, and Andrez from Damage's birthday party was wicked. I don't go to as many these days though, I've got a bit more selective because I'm tired a lot of the time.

Duncan: It's nice to go to a big celeb party sometimes, but it's also nice to just go and spend quality time with my friends and hang out.

Lee: I'm not a big one for going to the parties. When we first started I loved them, but I like chilling out now. But having said that, some of them are really good!

discography

Album: ALL RISE
Released: November 26th 2001
Album Chart: Peaked at No. 2

Reached Double Platinum in the UK within 6 weeks of release

Single: ALL RISE
Released: May 21st 2001
Singles Chart: Entered at No. 4

Stayed in the top 10 for 5 weeks

Single: TOO CLOSE
Released: August 27th 2001
Singles Chart: Entered at No. 1

Sold in excess of 200,000 copies

Is fame what you expected?
Antony: Yes.

Lee: No. But then I'm not what I expected.

Duncan: I agree.

Simon: Yes, pretty much. There are a lot of rumours about bands not getting on and stuff, but we all get on with each other really well. All the bands hang out together, which is really nice.

Single: IF YOU COME BACK
Released: November 12th 2001
Singles Chart: Entered at No. 1

Sold in excess of 200,000 copies

Single: FLY BY
Released: March 18th 2002
Singles Chart: Entered at No. 6

Remix of the album version

Limited edition DVD single: FLY BY
Released: March 18th 2002
Singles Chart: Entered at No. 1

Includes video, gallery and behind the scenes footage

What was your favourite member of Blue like as a young boy? Did they behave themselves at school? And how do they feel about being in Blue? You can find all the answers here!

Full name:	Lee Ryan
DOB:	17/6/1983
Height:	5' 11"
Brothers and sisters:	1 sister
From:	South East London
Hair colour:	Blond
Eye colour:	Green / Blue
Star sign:	Gemini

leeprofile

> ## "I think I was a nightmare for my mum growing up. I was always very lively."

IN THE BEGINNING

Lee is the youngest member of the band, but while he may look angelic, he reveals that when he was a kid he gave his mum some severe headaches with his manic behaviour.

"I think I was a nightmare for my mum growing up. I was always very

lively and we'd be in shops and I'd be running all over the place causing havoc. She'd have to spend ages looking for me while trying to do her shopping at the same time. I was quite a handful and very cheeky, and she'd have to have eyes in the back of her head to keep me in check.

My earliest memory is probably when I was in my pram, and I also remember learning to ride a bike clearly. I think I must have been about four. I was pretty good actually, and I didn't fall off too many times. Although I do remember crashing into a wall once though when I'd just learnt, which wasn't a lot of fun."

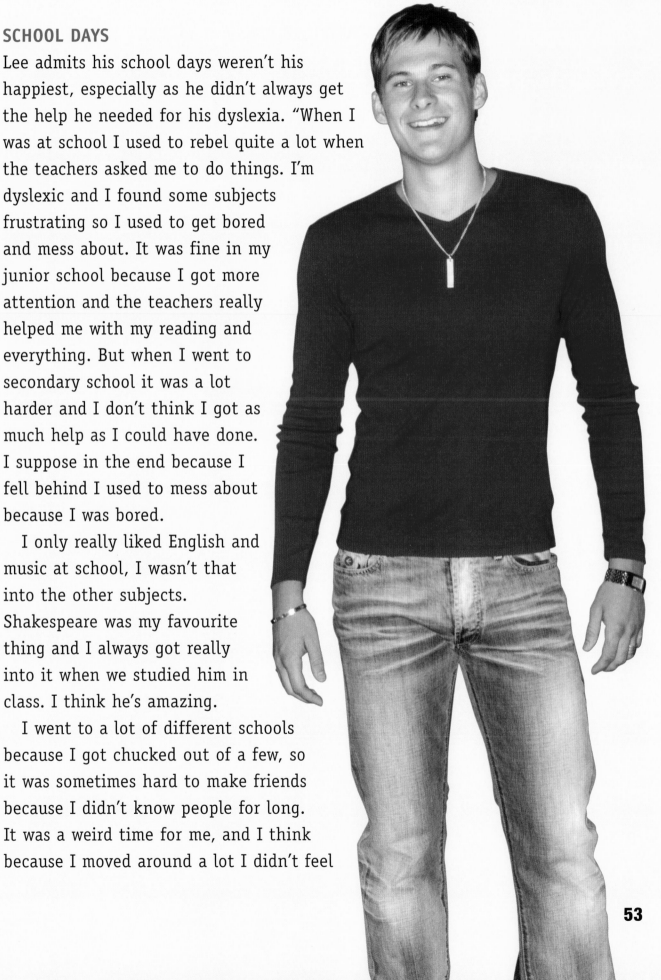

SCHOOL DAYS

Lee admits his school days weren't his happiest, especially as he didn't always get the help he needed for his dyslexia. "When I was at school I used to rebel quite a lot when the teachers asked me to do things. I'm dyslexic and I found some subjects frustrating so I used to get bored and mess about. It was fine in my junior school because I got more attention and the teachers really helped me with my reading and everything. But when I went to secondary school it was a lot harder and I don't think I got as much help as I could have done. I suppose in the end because I fell behind I used to mess about because I was bored.

I only really liked English and music at school, I wasn't that into the other subjects. Shakespeare was my favourite thing and I always got really into it when we studied him in class. I think he's amazing.

I went to a lot of different schools because I got chucked out of a few, so it was sometimes hard to make friends because I didn't know people for long. It was a weird time for me, and I think because I moved around a lot I didn't feel

53

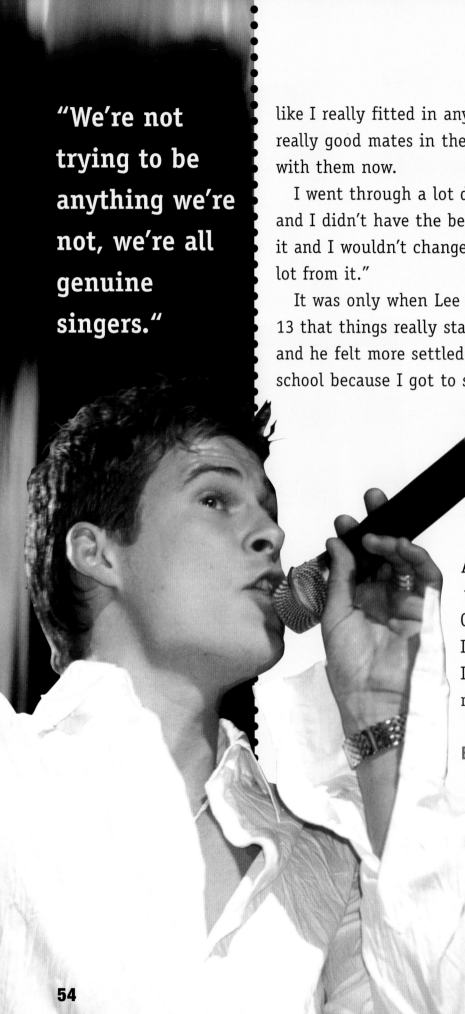

> **"We're not trying to be anything we're not, we're all genuine singers."**

like I really fitted in anywhere. But I did make some really good mates in the end, and I'm still friends with them now.

I went through a lot during my early school days and I didn't have the best time, but I came through it and I wouldn't change things because I learnt a lot from it."

It was only when Lee went to drama school aged 13 that things really started to take off for him and he felt more settled. "I really enjoyed drama school because I got to sing and act and stuff, so I had more to concentrate on. I enjoyed the acting side even more than the singing at that time, and I remember playing the Artful Dodger in *Oliver* at the Bloomsbury Theatre in Central London and loving it. I still really enjoy acting and I wouldn't mind doing some more one day."

BOY IN BLUE

Despite his love of acting, for now Lee is more than happy to concentrate on his thriving singing career. "I've always loved singing, but I was never looking to get into a boy band particularly. I wasn't fussy about what I wanted to do. My mum always really encouraged me with my singing and it kind of spurred me on, and obviously I'm really happy with how things have turned out.

Antony, Duncan and Simon have all got real talent and they can all sing really well which I think is the most important thing about Blue. I never wanted to be in a band where we were selling ourselves on an image and there was no talent to back it up. We're not trying to be anything we're not, we're all genuine singers and what you see is what you get.

I don't know what I'd be doing if I wasn't in Blue. I haven't really thought about it. As far as I'm concerned I'm here and I'm happy. It's wicked."

Lee questionsand

Lee reveals that he loves his dictaphone and his lie-ins, and hopes to be settled down with kids in 20 years' time...

What did you get for your last birthday?
My record company gave me a Gucci shirt, which was cool.

Do you give to charity?
Yes, I think it's important.

Cats or dogs?
Either, I'm not that bothered. But I used to have a cat when I was younger.

Who was the last person you spoke to on the phone?
My mum.

What's your worst household chore?
I'm very good at ironing and hoovering, I don't mind doing that at all, but I absolutely hate washing up and will do anything to get out of doing it. I just hate it.

answers

"We always have a laugh."

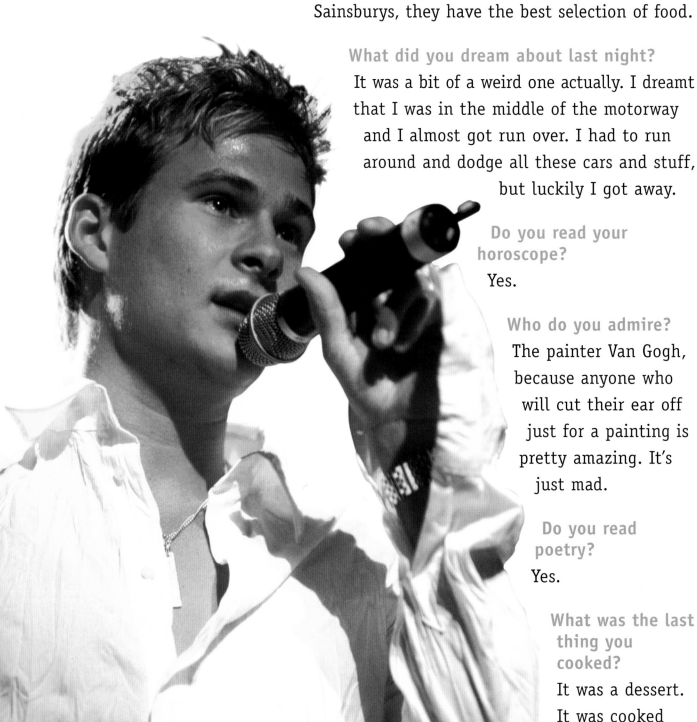

How do you end your phone calls?
I say "Spanish". It means "Spanish waiter" which is rhyming slang for later.

Where do you do your grocery shopping?
Sainsburys, they have the best selection of food.

What did you dream about last night?
It was a bit of a weird one actually. I dreamt that I was in the middle of the motorway and I almost got run over. I had to run around and dodge all these cars and stuff, but luckily I got away.

Do you read your horoscope?
Yes.

Who do you admire?
The painter Van Gogh, because anyone who will cut their ear off just for a painting is pretty amazing. It's just mad.

Do you read poetry?
Yes.

What was the last thing you cooked?
It was a dessert. It was cooked

pears with pistachio nuts and orange, and I made a sauce to go over the top using sugar, cream, orange juice, coconut cream, and grated coconut. It was very nice actually.

What time do you sleep in until when you've got a day off?
About 12, I like a lie-in.

What's in your fridge?
Nothing at the moment because I've been away.

What's in your pockets?
My dictaphone – so I can record melodies and stuff whenever I have ideas when I'm travelling around – and my phone.

What will you be doing in 20 years' time?

I'll be settled down with kids, definitely.

When did you last laugh until you cried?
I don't know. Probably with the lads, we always have a laugh.

What was the first single you ever bought?
How Come, How Long by Stevie Wonder and Babyface.

What's the most romantic thing you've ever done?
Probably cooking dinner for a girl.

Do you believe in aliens?
Yes.

What's your duvet like?
Blue.

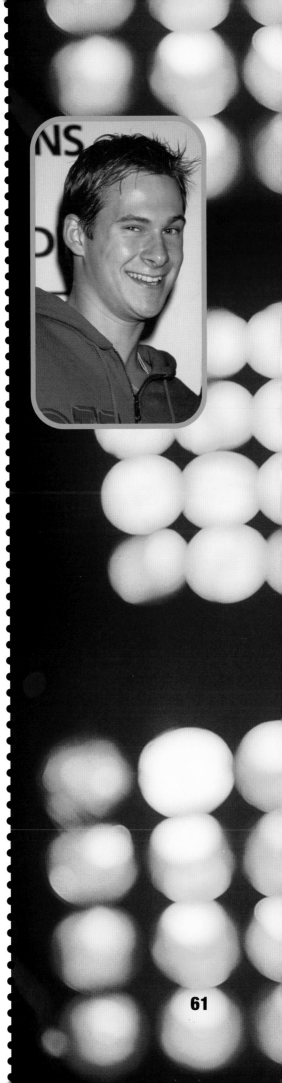

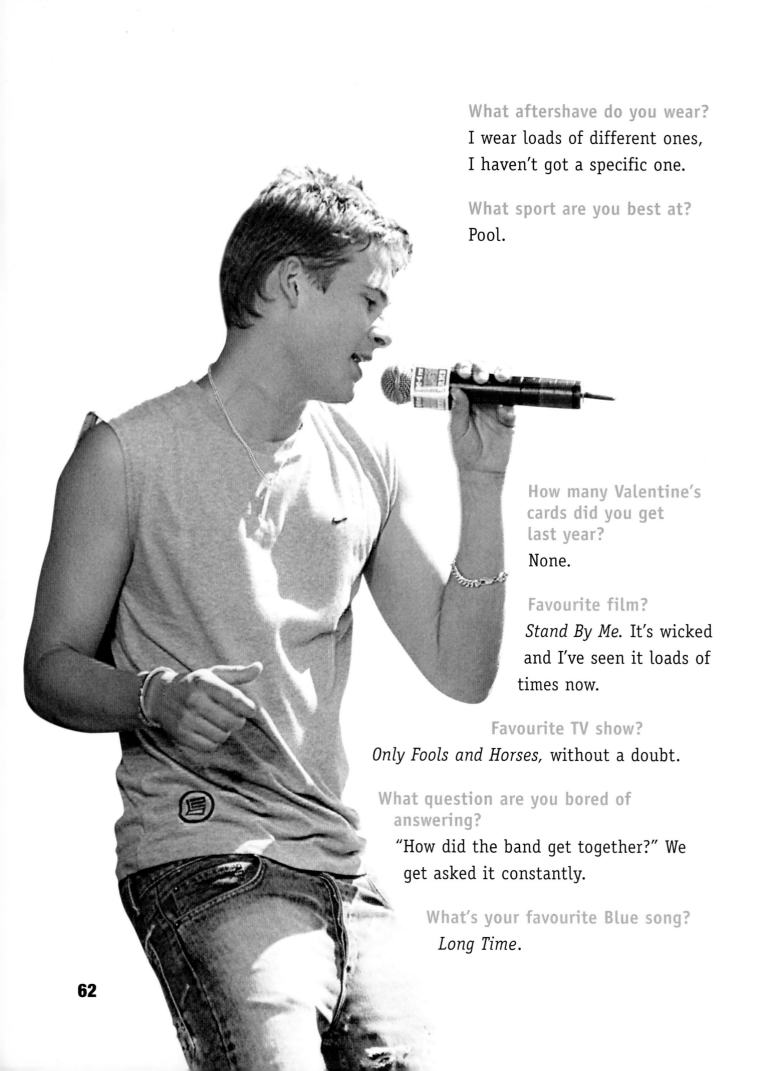

What aftershave do you wear?
I wear loads of different ones,
I haven't got a specific one.

What sport are you best at?
Pool.

**How many Valentine's
cards did you get
last year?**
None.

Favourite film?
Stand By Me. It's wicked
and I've seen it loads of
times now.

Favourite TV show?
Only Fools and Horses, without a doubt.

**What question are you bored of
answering?**
"How did the band get together?" We
get asked it constantly.

What's your favourite Blue song?
Long Time.

Who would you most like to work with?
Babyface.

Where do you buy your clothes?
Anywhere that's got nice stuff, I'm not that fussy.

Favourite food?
Sushi.

Where did you go on your last holiday?
Scotland, and before that it was St. Lucia.

What's your biggest extravagance?
Clothes. I definitely spend most of my money on clothes.

Which five people – dead or alive – would you invite to your fantasy dinner party?
Marilyn Monroe, Ghandi, Muhammad Ali, Mother Theresa and Lee Evans. So if I got bored of being serious, Lee Evans could make me laugh.

Are you allergic to anything?
No.

What do you usually do on a Saturday night out?
I like to stay in and cook a meal. I enjoy doing that these days.

All Rise!

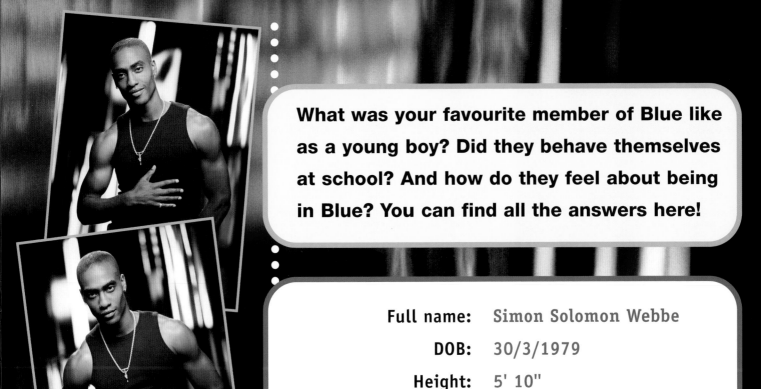

What was your favourite member of Blue like as a young boy? Did they behave themselves at school? And how do they feel about being in Blue? You can find all the answers here!

Full name:	Simon Solomon Webbe
DOB:	30/3/1979
Height:	5' 10"
Brothers and sisters:	4 brothers and 2 sisters
From:	Manchester
Hair colour:	Black
Eye colour:	Brown
Star sign:	Aries

simonprofile

IN THE BEGINNING

"I was a spoilt kid, but I wasn't a brat," Simon insists as he starts filling us in on his childhood.

"My first memory is of my mum dropping me off at nursery. Unlike the other kids I didn't really notice that my mum was leaving – I've always had a short attention span – I just turned around and started playing with these kids and didn't cry or anything. Then at lunchtime I remember sitting down at this table and being really, really hungry, so when the teacher turned away I grabbed something and put it in my mouth. It turned out to be egg which I'm allergic to, so I had to spit it out, and that's when I started crying because I realised my mum wasn't about."

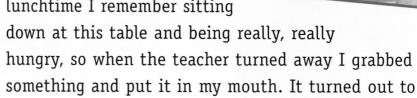

SCHOOL DAYS

Thankfully things soon improved, and throughout his school days Simon was a keen (and impressive) athlete. And as he explains, he always used his muscles in a positive way.

"My favourite subject at school was PE. I was always a physical child running around the playground playing games and I absolutely loved football. I wasn't very good academically. I suppose I didn't see the point because I was too into my sport.

"My favourite subject at school was PE."

I was the kid at school who hated bullies, so I'd always stick up for anyone that was being bullied. I wasn't a naughty child as such. My mum always drummed it into me to have manners and never talk back to my elders, so I never really got into trouble. My school reports said I was an excellent child and I had 100 per cent attendance. I was head boy as well. I was already captain of the football team so I think the teachers thought I was a good role model."

Simon showed a keen interest in performing early on, but because his love of football always came first, he didn't even consider a career on the stage until his late teens. "I always got the lead parts in plays at school, and drama was always one of my favourite subjects. I was once the main part in a play called *Days of my Childhood*, and I remember after one show this guy came up to me and said: 'You're not going to be a professional footballer, you're going to be on the stage entertaining people'. I didn't recognise him at first, but it turned out that he was the guy who first spotted me playing football when I was nine and became my first manager. I didn't think that much of it at the time because I never expected to be doing this, but now I think about what he said every time I get up on the stage. So thank you, George!"

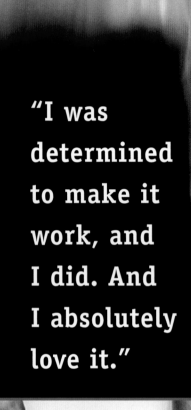

> "I was determined to make it work, and I did. And I absolutely love it."

BOY IN BLUE

Sadly, despite being signed to Port Vale and later being poached by Stoke City, Simon's dreams of becoming a professional footballer crumbled when he was injured, and it was then that he started to think seriously about becoming a performer.

"I got injured when I got kicked playing football when I was 19, and damaged the ligaments in both my ankles. I didn't pass my medical and my doctor told me I wouldn't be able to play professional football for a while. All I could do was rest and it was so hard because since the age of nine I'd been kicking a ball around and I didn't know anything else.

For the first time in my life I almost cried thinking I might never be able to play football professionally, and I started trying to decide what to do with my life. I started to feel really sorry for myself, and so in the end I started going to the gym every day to give myself something to do.

A little while later this woman I knew asked me to enter a modelling competition called The Face of '98 for a black woman's magazine called *Pride*. To cut a long story short, I won the whole thing and got a modelling contract in London.

I moved to London and during that time I must have met every r 'n' b and rap artist going, and decided that that was what I wanted to do. So I started channelling all my energies into rapping.

I had been to a few auditions for things, and it was at one that I met Lee and he

later told me about Blue. I'd already been working on solo stuff, and I remember when I told my mum about this band she was really worried because I'd been let down with the football stuff in the past. I think she's very protective of me because I'm her first child, but I was in a wonderland and was so sure the band was going to work out. I was determined to make it work, and I did. And I absolutely love it."

Si questionsand

Simon would like to climb a mountain, will shop anywhere, and is very good at cleaning. But that's not all we found out...

What did you get for your last birthday?
A Versace ring and matching earrings, which I wore in the video for *If You Come Back*.

Do you give to charity?
Yes.

Cats or dogs?
Neither.

Who was the last person you spoke to on the phone?
Our manager, Daniel Glatman.

What's your worst household chore?
None really, I'm quite clean. I'm quite good around the house and there's nothing I really hate doing.

answers

"Don't do it if it doesn't make you happy".

How do you end your phone calls?
"One".

Where do you do your grocery shopping?
Anywhere, I'm not fussy about brands and stuff.

What did you dream about last night?
I usually always remember my dreams, but I didn't have one last night.

Do you read your horoscope?
No, I stopped when we got our record deal because I want to let fate take it's path now. I always used to read them, but I don't believe that they're that accurate. I think you can relate what they say to just about anybody.

How long does it take you to get ready for a night out?
45 minutes to an hour. I don't like rushing, I like to take my time and chill out and moisturise and everything.

Do you read poetry?
No.

What book changed your life?
None, but I'm reading a book at the moment called *The Power of Positive Thinking*. I've only just started it so I can't tell you what it's like.

What was the last thing you cooked?
A complete meal – chicken with rice and garlic potatoes.

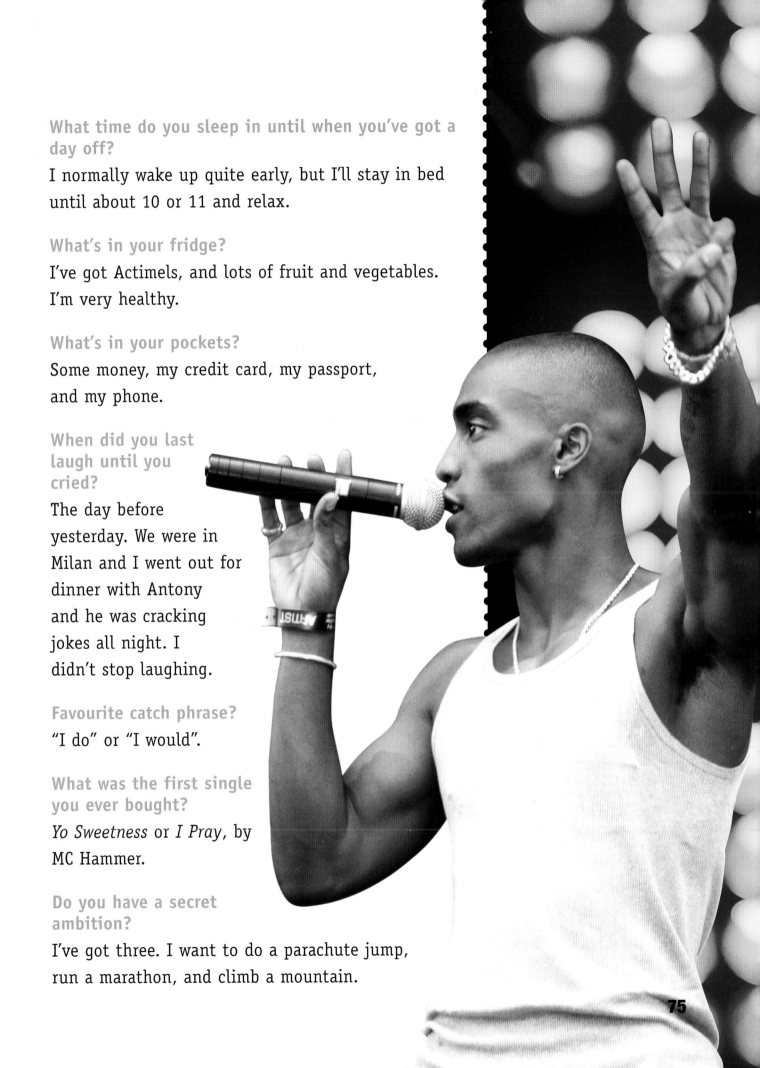

What time do you sleep in until when you've got a day off?

I normally wake up quite early, but I'll stay in bed until about 10 or 11 and relax.

What's in your fridge?

I've got Actimels, and lots of fruit and vegetables. I'm very healthy.

What's in your pockets?

Some money, my credit card, my passport, and my phone.

When did you last laugh until you cried?

The day before yesterday. We were in Milan and I went out for dinner with Antony and he was cracking jokes all night. I didn't stop laughing.

Favourite catch phrase?

"I do" or "I would".

What was the first single you ever bought?

Yo Sweetness or *I Pray*, by MC Hammer.

Do you have a secret ambition?

I've got three. I want to do a parachute jump, run a marathon, and climb a mountain.

What's the most romantic thing you've ever done?

I took a girl to Mexico on holiday.

What's your motto for life?

"Don't do it if it doesn't make you happy".

What's your duvet like?

It's cream.

What aftershave do you wear?

Loads, Gucci Rush, Armani... name anything and I've got it.

What sport are you best at?

Football.

How many Valentine's cards did you get last year?

None.

Favourite film?

Belly, with DMX, Nars and T-Boz from TLC. It's a gangster film.

Favourite TV show?

Friends and *Smallville*.

What question are you bored of answering?

Whenever we go to a new country they ask us what we think of it, even though we've only just got there and we haven't had a chance to see the place!

Which five people, dead or alive, would you invite to your fantasy dinner party?

Muhammad Ali, Bob Marley, Biggie Smalls, Tupac and Zhang Ziyi, the woman from *Rush Hour 2*.

What's the best advice you've ever been given by anyone?

Sometimes you've got to be cruel to be kind.

What's your favourite Blue song?

Long Time.

Who would you most like to work with?

112.

How do you keep in shape?

I don't, I don't have time to go to the gym anymore. But if I could I'd go three or four times a week.

Where did you go on your last holiday?

Mexico.

What's your biggest extravagance?

Clothes.

Are you allergic to anything?

Eggs.

All Rise!

thequestionsthey didn'twantustoask!

all bands get asked dodgy questions from time to time, and in the name of research, we asked Blue a choice selection...

If you could change anything about yourself, what would it be?

Lee: My nose. I don't like my nose at all.

Simon: I think I'd change my awareness because sometimes I can be inconsiderate to people without knowing it.

Duncan: My nose. It's got a bump on it from where I've broken it and I can't breathe through my right nostril properly. I've got a complex about my nose because I think it's too big.

Antony: I've got a bit of a hairy chest, and also my eyes are a bit droopy like Sylvester Stallone's.

What's the longest you've gone without changing your socks?

Duncan: I have to change my socks every day.

Antony: Two days.

Lee: A couple of days.

Simon: Three days.

When did you last get told off and what was it for?

Antony: About a month ago when I came in really late from a club and woke my mum up. She's given me a set of keys now.

Lee: I got told off for being late. That happens quite a lot because I'm not very good with my time keeping.

Duncan: My mum told me off yesterday because I had a bit of a big night out on Saturday and I felt terrible. I'd promised to help her with something but I felt too ill.

Simon: My mum told me off for getting another tattoo. It's of a snake because that was my nickname at school.

What's the dodgiest haircut you've ever had?

Lee: I had a bowl haircut when I was younger, and it was quite a long bowl as well.

Simon: I haven't had any really bad ones actually. I've always moved with the times.

Duncan: My friend Rita's boyfriend Theo is a hairdresser. He asked me to be in this hair show and gave me this flat-top with different coloured circles around it. It looked wicked for the show, but I had to live with it afterwards and it wasn't very me.

Antony: When I went on *Surprise, Surprise* and did *Grease* my hair looked awful. My hair is naturally curly so it went a bit mad.

When was the last time you totally embarrassed yourself?

Antony: When I was drunk and I was talking utter rubbish to my mate's dad. I was so embarrassed afterwards.

Simon: I'm very careful not to embarrass myself. I'm really aware of what I do all the time.

Lee: I always embarrass myself, especially as I'm quite bad at saying stuff without thinking.

Duncan: I embarrass myself quite a lot actually, I do stupid things. I remember when my friend Phil pulled my tracksuit bottoms down in the middle of a supermarket. I had nothing on underneath and had to stand there exposed to everyone. I couldn't do anything but laugh.

If you were invisible for a day, who would you spy on?

Duncan: I don't think I'd spy on anyone in particular, I'd just take advantage of the fact that I was invisible and freak people out.

Antony: I want to go into a girl's toilet and find out what they talk about and why they always have to go to the loo in pairs.

Lee: I think I'd go and spy on the government, or I'd go to Area 51. It would be fascinating to find out what really goes on.

Simon: Zhang Ziyi from *Rush Hour 2*.

Have you ever been denied entry anywhere?

Antony: A few places, but it doesn't bother me at all.

Duncan: I used to get denied entry everywhere when I was 18 because I looked really young. I also used to get pulled over by the police all the time because I didn't look old enough to drive.

Simon: Oh yeah, loads of places. But nowadays people who used to turn me away say hello and act like they're my mates. That does my head in.

Lee: I have done loads of times but I'd never say: "Don't you know who I am?"

What's the worst knockback you've had from a girl?

Simon: When I was ten a girl said she didn't want to go out with me because I was black. She was only young and she's one of my best mates now.

Lee: I don't know. I'm quite chatty with girls and I'll talk to anyone, so it doesn't bother me if a girl gives me the brush off. I just move on.

Antony: A girl once said to me: "You're short, aren't you?"

Duncan: I had a crush on this girl for three years at school and we eventually kissed one night. But then when I asked her out afterwards she said no. I was devastated.